Great Women in History

Marie Curie

by Erin Edison

Consulting Editor: Gail Saunders-Smith, PhD

CAPSTONE PRESS
a capstone imprint

Pebble Books are published by Capstone Press,
1710 Roe Crest Drive, North Mankato, Minnesota 56003.
www.capstonepub.com

Library of Congress Cataloging-in-Publication Data
Edison, Erin.
  Marie Curie / by Erin Edison.
      pages cm.—(Pebble books. Great women in history)
  Includes bibliographical references and index.
  Summary: "Describes the life and work of scientist Marie Cure"—Provided by
publisher.
    ISBN 978-1-4765-4216-4 (library binding)—ISBN 978-1-4765-5164-7 (paperback)—
ISBN 978-1-4765-6021-2 (ebook PDF)
  1. Curie, Marie, 1867-1934—Juvenile literature. 2. Chemists—Poland—Biography—
Juvenile literature. 3. Women chemists—Poland—Biography—Juvenile literature. 4.
Chemists—France—Biography—Juvenile literature. 5. Women chemists—France—
Biography—Juvenile literature. I. Title.
  QD22.C8E35 2014
  540.92—dc23 [B]   2013030096

Editorial Credits
Erika L. Shores, editor; Gene Bentdahl, designer; Marcie Spence, media researcher;
Laura Manthe, production specialist

Photo Credits
Alamy Images: World History Archive, cover; Getty Images: AFP, 6, Popperfoto,
20, Universal History Archive, 4, 16, 18; Newscom: Keystone Pictures USA/ZUMA
Press, 1, Prisma, 12, World History Archive, 8, 10, 14

Note to Parents and Teachers

The Great Women in History set supports national social studies standards related
to people and culture. This book describes and illustrates Marie Curie. The images
support early readers in understanding the text. The repetition of words and phrases
helps early readers learn new words. This book also introduces early readers to
subject-specific vocabulary words, which are defined in the Glossary section. Early
readers may need assistance to read some words and to use the Table of Contents,
Glossary, Read More, Internet Sites, and Index sections of the book.

Printed in the United States of America in North Mankato, Minnesota.
092013   007764CGS14

Table of Contents

Early Life. 5
Life's Work 11
Later Life. 17

Glossary 22
Read More 23
Internet Sites. 23
Critical Thinking Using the
Common Core 24
Index 24

1867

born

Early Life

Marie Curie was a famous scientist.

She was born in Poland in 1867.

Her parents were school teachers.

Marie had three sisters and

one brother.

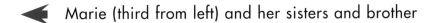
Marie (third from left) and her sisters and brother

1867 born

1891 moves to Paris

1895 marries

In 1891 Marie moved to Paris, France.

She studied math and physics.

Marie was the best student in her class.

In 1895 Marie married a scientist

named Pierre Curie.

 Pierre Curie and Marie in 1895

1867
born

1891
moves to
Paris

1895
marries

Marie and Pierre worked together

in a science laboratory in Paris.

They had two daughters.

Irène was born in 1897.

Ève was born in 1904.

 Marie and her daughters in 1908

1867
born

1891
moves to
Paris

1895
marries

Life's Work

Marie taught classes in Paris and did science experiments. She studied elements. These substances make up everything in nature. Marie found that only certain elements give off rays of energy. Marie called this radioactivity.

1867
born

1891
moves to
Paris

1895
marries

1898
discovers polonium
and radium

In 1898 Marie and Pierre discovered two new elements. They named them polonium and radium. Radium was extremely radioactive. Doctors found radium helpful for treating cancer.

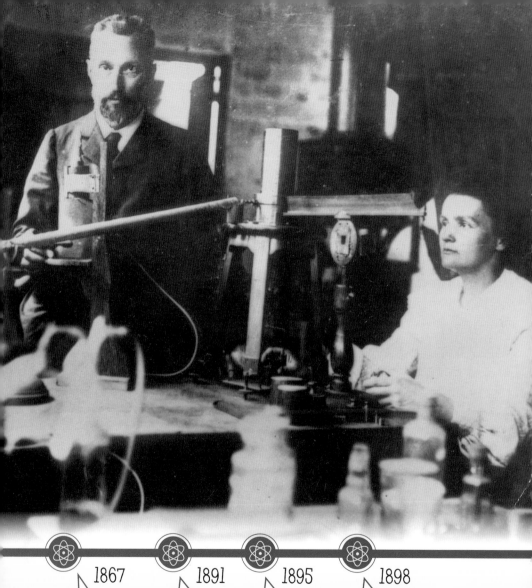

In 1903 Marie and Pierre won
the Nobel Prize in physics for
their work with radium.
Sadly, Pierre died in an accident
in 1906.

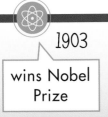

1903
wins Nobel
Prize

1867 — born

1891 — moves to Paris

1895 — marries

1898 — discovers polonium and radium

Later Life

Marie kept working in their lab.
In 1911 she won the Nobel
Prize in chemistry. She was
the first person to win
two Nobel Prizes.

Marie's daughter Irène (left) was also a scientist.

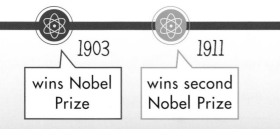

1903
wins Nobel
Prize

1911
wins second
Nobel Prize

 1867
born

 1891
moves to Paris

1895
marries

 1898
discovers polonium and radium

Marie started the Radium Institute

at the University of Paris in 1914.

Scientists there studied ways

to use radium.

Irène and Marie at the Radium Institute in 1919

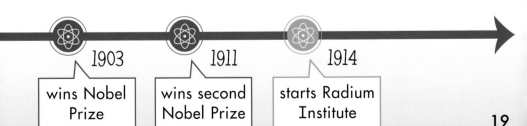

1903
wins Nobel
Prize

1911
wins second
Nobel Prize

1914
starts Radium
Institute

1867
born

1891
moves to
Paris

1895
marries

1898
discovers polonium
and radium

Marie died in 1934.

People remember her as

a great scientist. Scientists at

the Radium Institute continue

her work today.

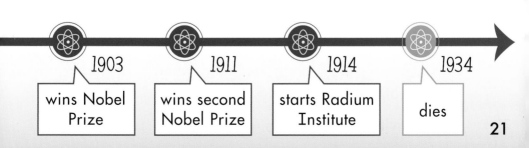

1903
wins Nobel
Prize

1911
wins second
Nobel Prize

1914
starts Radium
Institute

1934
dies

Glossary

cancer—a serious disease in which some cells in the body grow faster than normal cells

chemistry—the branch of science dealing with the study of substances, what they are made up of, and the ways they react with each other

element—a substance that cannot be broken down into simpler substances

energy—the ability to do work, such as giving off heat or light

experiment—a scientific test to find out how something works

institute—a school or group that is set up for a special purpose

laboratory—a room where scientists do experiments

Nobel Prize—an award given each year for work in the fields of physics, chemistry, literature, physiology or medicine, and peace

physics—the study of matter and energy, including light, heat, electricity, and motion

radioactivity—the process of giving off rays

Read More

Lin, Yoming S. *The Curies and Radioactivity.* Eureka! New York: PowerKids Press, 2012.

Lindeen, Mary. *Marie Curie: Scientist.* Edina, Minn.: Magic Wagon, 2009.

Venezia, Mike. *Marie Curie: Scientist Who Made Glowing Discoveries.* Getting to Know the World's Greatest Inventors and Scientists. New York: Children's Press, 2009.

Internet Sites

FactHound offers a safe, fun way to find Internet sites related to this book. All of the sites on FactHound have been researched by our staff.

Here's all you do:

Visit *www.facthound.com*

Type in this code: 9781476542164

Check out projects, games and lots more at
www.capstonekids.com

Critical Thinking Using the Common Core

1. How did Marie's work with elements lead to her discovery of radioactivity? (Key Ideas and Details)

2. Look at the timeline on pages 16 and 17. What does that tell you about Marie's discoveries and the awards she won as a result? (Craft and Structure)

Index

birth, 5
cancer, 13
chemistry, 17
Curie, Ève, 9
Curie, Irène, 9
Curie, Pierre, 7, 9, 13, 15
death, 21
elements, 11, 13
experiments, 11
laboratories, 9, 17
marriage, 7

math, 7
Nobel Prizes, 15, 17
parents, 5
Paris, 7, 9, 11, 19
physics, 7, 15
polonium, 13
radioactivity, 11, 13
radium, 13, 15, 19
Radium Institute, 19, 21
siblings, 5
teaching, 11

Word Count: 226
Grade: 1
Early-Intervention Level: 24